3-D THRILL

ICE AGE

A n ice age is when the world's temperature drops and stays low for a long period of time and ice spreads out from the poles. Throughout history there have been lots of ice ages. But when people talk about the Ice Age they mean the one that began around 2.5 million years ago and lasted until about 10,000 years ago.

MAKE YOUR MIND UP

When people think of the Ice Age they think of snow, cold weather and strange shaggy beasts. It's true that at times, great sheets of ice covered a lot of the Earth's surface; but this is only part of the story. At other times it was quite mild and the ice sheets would retreat north and the temperature would rise before things started to cool down again.

WHAT CAUSED THE ICE AGE?

The Earth gets its warmth from the Sun. Any slight variation in the Earth's orbit – that's the path it takes as it goes round the sun – can lead to big variations in the temperature. Also, sometimes the Earth leans a little bit closer to or a little bit further away from the Sun, which can result in the Earth heating up a bit or cooling down. During the last Ice Age, the northern hemisphere of the Earth was probably tilted a little bit further away than normal and the result was that things got a little bit chilly.

AGE?

WHERE DID THEY GO?

The end of the Ice Age was remarkable on two fronts: firstly it got a lot warmer; secondly a lot of animals became extinct. No one is sure exactly why. Perhaps they were hunted to extinction? Perhaps they didn't like the warmer weather? Perhaps the vegetation changed too much? In short, we can't be sure.

Some scientists believe that we are still in the Ice Age but it doesn't feel cold because we're in one of the warmer periods.

HERE COME THE HUMANS

Another notable feature of the Ice Age was the story of the humans. In the northern hemisphere a species called Homo heidelbergensis arrived first. They did well until the arrival of the Neanderthals who in turn flourished until our direct ancestors the Homo sapiens turned up. Why did the humans survive when lots of other animals didn't? Well, we had a lot going for us – we were adaptable, could work as a team, could fashion tools and had language. And there's a good chance that we were responsible for killing everything else off!

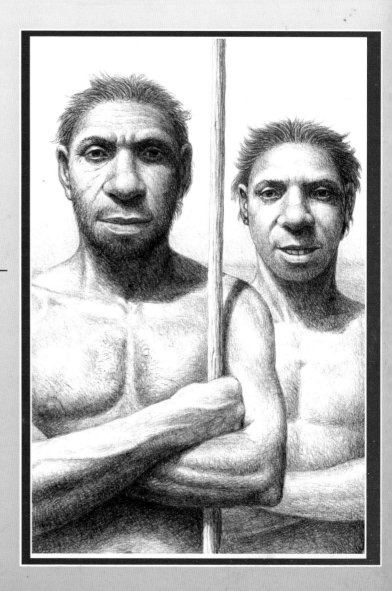

HAiRY BEASTS

If you're out and about in the cold it's a good idea to wrap up warm. That's precisely what many animals did during the Ice Age too. They grew thick shaggy coats to stop themselves freezing to death.

TiNY EARS

The mastodon might look like a mammoth, but it's a different species entirely. It had straighter tusks and different teeth which better suited its diet of tree leaves as opposed to grass. Like the mammoth, the mastodon had very small ears which helped it to cut back on the amount of heat it lost from its body. After all, it makes sense not to leave anything out in the cold that doesn't need to be there.

GRUMPY

A common sight across Europe was the woolly rhinoceros. This two-horned beast was a close relative of today's rare Sumatran rhinoceros. At around 3.5 metres long the woolly rhino was pretty big, but that was nothing compared to elasmotherium – another Ice Age rhino from Russia which was almost twice the size! Rhinos are well known for being a bit grumpy, so that was one animal it would have been wise to stay clear of.

WELL ADAPTED

One hairy creature that was particularly well-adapted to the freezing temperatures was the musk ox. Its shaggy coat was perfect for keeping the cold at bay. It was a survivor, too. Its direct relatives are still with us today – though they're not quite as big as their ancestors which were over half a metre taller.

Mammoths had a flap of skin that stopped cold air from getting up their bottoms.

SNOW PLOUGH

The one animal most people think of when you mention the Ice Age was the woolly mammoth. There were actually lots of different kinds of mammoth and not all of them were covered in shaggy fur. One common feature was the mammoths' huge, curved tusks. Scientists think that the mammoths used the tusks to push the snow away so they could get to the grass which they ate. In a way, mammoths were like hairy snow ploughs.

KILLERS IN THE COL[D]

Animals have been eating other animals for as long as creatures have taken a fancy to a bit of meat instead of leaves. That was true for the Ice Age too, which produced a bunch of carnivores that were fairly similar to the meat-eaters we have today — only bigger.

SMILEY

The most famous Ice Age carnivore was smilodon – the sabre toothed tiger. Smilodon wasn't actually related to today's tigers, but it was as large as the present day big cats and much stockier. Those huge fangs look pretty fearsome and they were handy for puncturing the skin of their prey, but they were no use at crunching through bone. This meant that smilodons had to leave most of the meat on their kills as they couldn't eat it without risking damaging their precious teeth – so no juicy ribs for these cats!

BALDY

The largest lion to have walked the planet terrorised plant-eaters and unsuspecting carnivores alike across Ice Age Europe. It was called the cave lion and at around 3 metres long it was considerably bigger than today's lions. However, male cave lions didn't have manes – strange, as you'd think you'd want as much hair as possible in the cold.

SHORT AND LONG

The biggest meat-eater of the Ice Age was the short-faced bear. Its face may have been on the short side for a bear, but everything else about this prehistoric teddy was huge. When it stood on its hind legs it would have been around 3 metres tall – easily bigger than today's largest bear, the polar bear. But was this giant a killer? Some people suggest that the short-faced bear was actually a scavenger and that it may well have munched on berries too, like today's bears do.

The biggest predator on land was a wolf-like animal called Andrewsarchus. It lived in what is now Mongolia and was around 5 metres long!

DIRE STRAITS

One common Ice Age predator was the dire wolf. These beasts were similar to their modern-day counterparts but were a bit larger. The good news for their prospective victims was that they had shorter legs than today's wolves, so they may not have been as good at getting about. The bad news was that they hunted in packs, so if you got away from one, there was always a chance another one would get you. More bad news – they had really big teeth, too.

SUPER-SIZED

A feature of the Ice Age period was that many of the animals were a great deal bigger than they are now. Any animal weighing over 44 kilograms is classed as being megafauna, or a large animal; and the Ice Age had plenty of megafauna. Earth was the land of the giants.

GIANT LUMBERJACK

Animals which today we think of as being quite small often grew quite big during the Ice Age. Take the beaver for example, which grew to the size of a bear. Imagine the size of trees that toothy terror could chomp its way through!

SUPER SLOTH

These days sloths are those sleepy animals that spend most of their days doing as little as possible and hanging from the trees. It's not really laziness; keeping still stops them from being spotted by predators. In the Ice Age some sloths had a different way of keeping safe – they were just too big to try and attack. The biggest sloth of all was megatherium – it was around 6 metres long and weighed about as much as an elephant. It was way too large to live in the trees of course, but if any predator got too close it got a mighty whack from those powerful arms and sharp claws for its trouble.

BOING BOING

Megafauna could be found all around the world. Australia was home to giant kangaroos known as procoptodon. They stood around twice as tall as the present day kangaroos but had a very short face compared to today's beasts. Not that you would want to make jokes about it – another notable difference was the large claw at the end of each foot!

Glyptodon was a kind of armadillo that was the size of a small car!

IRISH GIANT

Today's male deer, or stags as they are called, grow antlers on their heads. The more impressive the antlers, the more likely they are to mate. However, even the most impressive of today's antlers would look a little weedy when compared to those of megaloceros, sometimes known as the Irish elk. Their antlers could measure over 3.5 metres across, but this isn't really surprising as the deer itself was around 2 metres tall, making it the largest deer ever to have lived. Unfortunately it also seems to have been very tasty as it appears it was hunted to extinction around 7,500 years ago.

IT'S NOT UNUNSUAL

A s the climate during the Ice Age varied so much from warm to cold, the types of animals that could be found in just one area could change massively over time. As things got hotter or colder, the types of animal that lived there would change, leading to some surprising results.

GETTING THE HUMP

You would generally think of camels living somewhere quite dry and dusty, but until around 11,000 years ago they also lived across America! Remains that have been found suggest that this extinct version of the camel might have looked a bit like today's Bactrian camel – that's the one-humped variety to you and me. It may even have had no hump at all.

AHOY THERE

For many years it was thought that horses had been introduced to the USA by the Spanish after Columbus had arrived in 1492. In a way this story is correct, as there were no horses on the continent at that time. However, horses had been living in America since before the Ice Age. Around 10,000 years ago they either died out or moved away, possibly due to the changing climate. The next time America would see horses, they arrived by boat with the explorers.

JUST LIKE AFRICA

If you saw elephants wandering around and a hippopotamus in the river you could be fairly sure you were in Africa – unless you were in the Ice Age, then you could be in London! Over 120,000 years ago this would have been an everyday sight across much of Britain, but it's safe to say you don't get many hippos in the Thames these days.

The USA had its own version of a cheetah. It was called miracinonyx and was probably the speediest predator about.

TINY TUSKER

Although many Ice Age animals were bigger than their modern-day counterparts, not all were – some were even smaller. There was a small version of mammoth that lived in what is now the Californian Channel Islands in the USA. It was only 1.7 metres tall at the shoulder, which would make it shorter than many adult humans. This example of pygmy versions of animals isn't that rare either. It seems that sometimes animals adjust their size to their surroundings, so a small island leads to small animals.

HUMAN BEHAVIOUR

It's easy to think that our ancient ancestors were simple folk. The image of a caveman is someone who wears animal furs, carries a club and grunts a lot. However, the people of the Ice Age were a lot more sophisticated than that and their ability to survive is testament to their intelligence.

OBSOLETE OR MURDERED?

Neanderthals were one branch of the human family tree that was well-adapted to living in the Ice Age. They were short and stocky which helped to keep them warm. It also turns out that, as well as being very strong, they were much more intelligent than scientists used to believe. However, about 28,000 years ago Neanderthals disappeared. It was believed that they were unable to adapt to warmer conditions, but new finds dispute this. It now seems likely that they were wiped out by competing Homo sapiens.

THE WINNER IS...

The end of the Ice Age saw the arrival of our very own ancestors, the Homo sapiens. Compared to the Neanderthals our forbears were taller and slimmer with longer limbs. This made them better suited to moving around the no-longer frozen landscape. Also, Homo sapiens made finer tools and weapons than their Neanderthal cousins and would later develop farming techniques. It may well have been this all-round ability that has seen our version of human hang about for so long.

VANDALS

One activity that Ice Age people indulged in has been very helpful for scientists and historians today. Our ancestors decorated the walls of caves with their own artwork, often showing hunting scenes and pictures of animals. This shows us today a small slice of what life was like during the Ice Age. These paintings are very precious – which is generally not the opinion people usually have when someone's put graffiti all over the walls.

Some scientists believe that modern humans are descended from as little as 10,000 ancient Homo sapiens!

EXTERMINATE

It was long thought that our ancestors had been responsible for killing off animals such as the mammoths. It's true that Ice Age people did hunt these beasts –favourite techniques included chasing them over cliffs or into specially dug pits – but they may not have been as destructive as we first thought. Some scientists now argue that the changing climate had more to do with the extinctions than people did.

HOW WE KNOW

Scientists and historians recreate what the past might have been like by looking at whatever might have survived from a particular time. Fortunately, there are loads of remains around from the Ice Age, so we have a pretty good idea how people and animals lived.

BACK FROM THE DEAD

Some mammoth remains are so well-preserved that it has led some scientists to believe that they might be able to bring mammoths back from the dead. The idea would be to take cells from the mammoths and cross them with cells from the mammoth's closest living relative, the Indian elephant. Theoretically it's possible, but in practice it's a very difficult proposition – and no one knows if it will work or if it's even a good idea!

Scientists know what mammoths ate because they have found the remains of their food inside the stomachs of frozen mammoths.

STICKY END

Asphalt is a naturally occurring sticky substance a bit like tar. At Rancho La Brea in the USA, great pools of asphalt have been trapping animals for hundreds of thousands of years. It's an unfortunate way to go for the poor creatures but it also means that their bones don't erode or get dispersed. As a result, the fossils found in La Brea are of an excellent quality. What's more, there are thousands of them – including wolves, mammoths and smilodons!

PERFECTLY PRESERVED

Imagine going for a walk and bumping into a mammoth. Well that's exactly what might happen if you were wandering around the frozen Russian tundra. The mammoths that have been found there aren't alive of course, but some are almost perfectly preserved. The tundra is cold and one big advantage of the cold is it preserves things – just like a freezer. The only difference is that it's unlikely you're going to find Ice Age beasts in your freezer.

PLANTING EVIDENCE

Across Europe and America there are caves where both people and animals have lived. These caves often provide invaluable information of what life was like as they not only contain bones – often the remains of meals – but also samples of pollen. The pollen tells us what kind of plants were growing at different times, which in turn gives us an idea of how warm or cold the weather was.

This edition published in 2007 by Arcturus Publishing Limited
26/27 Bickels Yard, 151–153 Bermondsey Street,
London SE1 3HA

Author: Paul Harrison
Editor: Fiona Tulloch

3D images by Pinsharp 3D Graphics

Picture credits:
AKG: page 12, bottom left; page 13, bottom right.
Corbis: page 2, bottom left; page 5, top and bottom; page 12, top
right.
FLPA: page 10, top right.
Getty Images: page 6; page 11, bottom.
Natural History Museum: page 9, bottom left.
Rex Features: page 2, top right; page 13, top right.
Science Photo Library: page 3, bottom right; page 4, top and
bottom; page 8.
TopFoto: page 14, bottom left.

Image on page 7 courtesy of the Indiana State Museum and Historic
Sites. Image on page 15 courtesy of Shropshire County Museum
Service.

Printed in China

ISBN: 978-1-84193-733-5